EMERGENCY!

CHEMICAL ACCIDENT

Alex Woolf

ARCTURUS

This edition first published in 2011 by Arcturus Publishing

Distributed by Black Rabbit Books
P.O. Box 3263
Mankato
Minnesota MN 56002

Printed in China

Library of Congress Cataloging-in-Publication Data

Woolf, Alex, 1964-
 Chemical accident / by Alex Woolf.
    p. cm. -- (Emergency!)
 Includes bibliographical references and index.
 ISBN 978-1-84837-951-0 (library binding : alk. paper)
1. Chemicals--Accidents--History--20th century--Juvenile literature. 2. Chemical spills--History--20th century--
Juvenile literature. 3. Industrial accidents--History--20th century--Juvenile literature. I. Title.
 TP150.A23W66 2012
 363.11'09--dc22
                                        2011006631

Series concept: Alex Woolf
Editor and picture researcher: Alex Woolf
Designer: Ian Winton

Picture credits
Corbis: 4 (Firefly Productions), 5 (Tamas Kovacs/epa), 6 (Yuriy Kalynyak/epa), 7 (Narong Sangnak/epa), 8
(Bettmann), 11 (Michael S. Yamashita), 13 (Jack Burlot/Apis/Sygma), 19 (Harish Tyagi/epa), 20 (Bettmann), 21
(Reinhard Krause/Reuters), 22 (Jacques Pavlovsky/Sygma), 24 (Pascal Le Segretain/Sygma), 25 (Reuters), 26
(China Daily/Reuters), cover and 27 (China Daily/Reuters), 29 (John Madere).
Getty Images: 9 (Gamma Keystone), 14 (Evening Standard/Hulton Archive), 15 (Wesley/Hulton Archive), 16 (AFP),
17 (AFP).
Rex Features: 23 (Sipa Press).
Shutterstock: 10 (kotomiti).

Cover picture: A worker is rescued following a blast at a chemical plant in the city of Yizhou, southern China, in
August 2008.

Supplier 03, Date 0411, Print Run 1047
SL001696US

Contents

Chemicals and their Dangers 4

Dealing with Chemical Spills 6

Texas City, Texas, 1947 8

Minamata, Japan, 1953–1966 10

Feyzin, France, 1966 12

Flixborough, UK, 1974 14

Seveso, Italy, 1976 16

Bhopal, India, 1984 18

Bhopal, India: Killer Cloud 20

Schweizerhalle, Switzerland, 1986 22

Toulouse, France, 2001 24

Guangxi, China, 2008 26

Learning the Lessons 28

Glossary 30

Further Information 31

Index 32

Chemicals and their Dangers

There came a deafening explosion and a huge fireball lit up the night sky. Residents in the nearby town rushed into the street to see fire and smoke spreading from the chemical factory. Many knew people who worked there and worried for their safety. What they didn't know was that the explosion had caused a leak of toxic chemicals into the river, contaminating the local water supply.

What are chemicals?

A chemical is any kind of pure substance. In other words, it is something made out of just one kind of molecule. A molecule is a group of atoms—the basic units of matter. Water is one example of a chemical. It is made of molecules containing two hydrogen atoms and one oxygen atom.

When different chemicals are mixed together, they react to form new compounds. Many of these compounds are synthetic—they are not found in nature.

The chemical industry

When some chemicals are mixed or heated they make new substances, many of which are useful to us. A vast number of the things we use in our everyday lives are made using chemicals. Soap, clothing, hair dye, food, medicine, cleaning products, pesticides, and fertilizer are all made using chemicals, and a whole industry is devoted to making them.

Accidents may happen

The factories that use chemicals to make things must store these chemicals somewhere. The chemicals are usually in liquid form, so they are stored in large tanks or vats. These chemicals are often highly reactive. If they leak, they might react with the air to form new chemicals, which could be poisonous or explosive. Sometimes this can lead to disaster.

AT-A-GLANCE

There are, on average, 4,500 chemical accidents in factories around the world every year. Of these, about 50 percent occur in the United States, and 30 percent in the European Union. Most of these accidents are very minor.

Source: ility Engineering, Tampere, Finland

Sometimes disasters happen. In October 2010, in Hungary, a reservoir containing chemical waste broke its banks. The poisonous sludge flooded three villages, killing four and injuring over 100.

Dealing with Chemical Spills

Chemicals are dangerous. They can explode or burn, causing death and destruction. They can also leak into the soil, the air, or the water supply, resulting in serious illness and even death for humans and wildlife, as well as long-term damage to the environment. It is therefore very important that chemicals be handled with care, and spills be dealt with quickly and efficiently.

Sounding the alarm

People who work at chemical factories are trained to follow certain procedures in the event of a spill. If they do not know what kind of chemical has leaked, they should call the fire department. If flammable liquid has spilled, they should remove anything that might ignite it such as naked flames or electric power sources. They should also order the evacuation of the site.

Chemical spills don't always happen in factories. This one, in Ukraine, occurred when a train carrying dangerous chemicals came off the tracks. The resulting fire released toxic fumes, injuring 20 people.

Controlling the spill

Liquid spills should be contained using sandbags, earth, or absorbent pads. The chemical must then be treated to make it safe. For example, acids can be weakened by mixing them with water. After this, the area should be washed thoroughly. Most chemical factories have special drains that lead directly to chemical treatment plants. Anyone exposed to toxic chemicals should immediately remove contaminated clothing and soak their skin in water.

In this exercise drill in Thailand, emergency workers practice rescuing injured people from a chemical spill. The rescuers are wearing personal protective equipment.

SAVING LIVES

People who work with hazardous chemicals are issued with personal protective equipment (PPE). This includes a respirator, which is a mask that filters out toxic fumes. Other essential items are gloves, eye protectors, and a chemical-resistant apron or gown.

Texas City, Texas, 1947

It was 8:10 AM on April 16, 1947. Longshoremen were in Hold 4 of the cargo ship *Grandcamp*, loading it with a consignment of ammonium nitrate fertilizer. Suddenly, one of them spotted smoke…

Leaking gas

The men threw jugs of water on the fire, but the ship's captain ordered them to secure the hatches and fill the hold with steam. Unfortunately, the steam heated up the ammonium nitrate, which started giving off flammable gases. As bright orange smoke poured from the ship, it attracted a crowd of curious onlookers.

Explosion!

At 9:12 AM, the ship exploded with such force that the shock wave knocked two small planes out of the sky. A giant cloud billowed 2,000 feet (600 m) into the air. The firefighters, dockyard workers, and bystanders near the ship were instantly killed. A giant wave surged inland, sweeping away all in its path. The ship's anchor, which weighed more than a ton, was flung 2 miles (3 km) inland. Other red-hot remnants of the *Grandcamp* showered the town for several more minutes, killing people, damaging property, and starting fires.

The explosion of the *Grandcamp* started fires all over the city, including this one at an oil refinery.

The horror continues

A nearby ship, *High Flyer*, also loaded with dangerous chemicals, had been damaged in the explosion. Later that day, people noticed flames coming from one of its holds. At 1:10 AM on April 17, *High Flyer* exploded with a blast even bigger than *Grandcamp*.

AT-A-GLANCE

Death toll: 581
Injured: Around 3,500
Property damage: Equivalent of around US$4.2 billion

RESCUE!

At 11 PM on April 16, two tugboats tried to pull the burning *High Flyer* away from the harbor and safely out to sea. A boarding party cut the anchor chain, but the tugs still couldn't move the ship, which had lodged itself against another vessel. At 1 PM, the tugs retrieved the boarders and made their escape—just minutes before the ship exploded!

Volunteers help to rescue survivors of the Texas City disaster.

Minamata, Japan, 1953–1966

Dr. Hosokawa of the Chisso Corporation factory hospital in Minamata was puzzled. One of his patients, a previously healthy five-year-old girl, was now struggling to walk and talk, and suffering frequent convulsions. The date was April 21, 1956. Over the next few days, ten more people began showing the same symptoms. On May 1, Dr. Hosokawa reported to the local public health office the outbreak of a previously unknown disease.

Cats and fish

The 1956 outbreak intensified people's fears that something was badly wrong in Minamata. The first signs had come in 1953, when the fish in the bay began to die. Then cats started falling into the sea. Soon people would stumble while walking and lose the ability to write or dress themselves.

EYEWITNESS

"At first our only hope was that she could walk. Then, we prayed that she could go to school. Now our hope is that she will be able to take care of herself when we no longer can."

The mother of Minamata disease sufferer Shinobu Sakamoto

For more than 30 years, the Chisso factory dumped mercury waste into Minamata Bay. Bacteria in the bay changed the mercury into the even more deadly chemical, methyl mercury.

Mercury poisoning

The main employer in the town of Minamata was the Chisso Corporation plastics factory. Since 1932 the factory had been dumping wastewater containing highly poisonous mercury into the bay. By 1959 researchers had proved that so-called "Minamata disease" was caused by people eating mercury-contaminated fish and shellfish. Despite this evidence, Chisso continued to pump mercury waste into Minamata Bay until 1966. By this time, more than a third of the town's population had left and its fishing industry was destroyed.

Victims of Minamata disease suffer from muscle weakness, numbness, and damage to their speech and hearing.

FORTY YEARS ON

The Japanese government officially blamed Chisso for Minamata disease in 1968. But it took until 1995 for the Japanese Supreme Court to find the company's directors guilty of causing the disaster. Chisso was ordered to pay 4.5 billion yen in compensation to victims of the disease.

Feyzin, France, 1966

On an icy morning in early January 1966, a routine operation was being carried out at the Elf oil refinery in Feyzin, France. A plant operator was taking a sample from one of the refinery's propane storage spheres. Unfortunately he opened the valves beneath the sphere in the wrong sequence...

Injury

When he opened the final valve, nothing happened. He opened it more fully, and a powerful jet of propane rushed out. The operator staggered backward, his arm and face in agony from the freezing liquid. As he fell, he partly pulled off the valve handle. The two men with him were unable to replace the valve handle and shut the valve. The pressure in the tank began to fall, causing the propane to boil and release clouds of highly flammable vapor.

Fire!

The men set off on foot to raise the alarm, fearing that if they drove, a spark from the engine might set fire to the gas. Meanwhile, the gas cloud spread 500 feet (150 m) to a nearby road where it was ignited by a car. The ruptured sphere was quickly enveloped in flames up to 200 feet (60 m) high.

AT-A-GLANCE

Death toll: 18

Injured: 81

Damage: 5 storage spheres destroyed

Evacuated from local town: 5,000

Fatal error

When firefighters arrived, they ignored the burning sphere, and instead used their hoses to cool the surrounding spheres. This was a mistake. After 90 minutes, the ruptured sphere exploded, killing and injuring several firefighters. The explosion damaged four other spheres, one of which also ruptured and later exploded. Several gasoline and crude oil tanks also caught fire. The fire took 48 hours to extinguish.

This photo, taken after the fire at the Feyzin refinery, shows one of the burned and damaged spheres.

BLEVE

The explosion at Feyzin was known as a BLEVE (boiling liquid expanding vapor explosion). This occurs when pressurized liquid inside a container reaches a temperature well above its atmospheric boiling point, causing it to explode.

SAVING LIVES

Since the Feyzin disaster, petrochemical plants have adopted much safer designs for pressurized tanks containing liquefied gases. Despite this, accidents have occurred since, and a number of firefighters have been killed in explosions. As a result, the policy now is complete evacuation of the area until the fire has burned itself out.

Flixborough, UK, 1974

Just after 4 PM on Saturday, June 1, 1974, a pipe caught fire at the Nypro Works chemical plant near Flixborough. The local fire department was summoned. At 4:53 PM, while the fire engines were still on their way, there was a massive explosion, loud enough to be heard more than 25 miles (40 km) away.

Disaster zone

When they arrived, the firefighters were confronted by a scene of devastation, with individual fires raging across a 65-acre (24-ha) area. The control room had collapsed, killing all 18 workers inside. Properties up to 5 miles (8 km) from the site suffered serious damage.

Firefighters at the scene of the Nypro chemical plant fire near Flixborough. Several suffered acid burn injuries while fighting the blaze.

SAVING LIVES

Firefighters organized the complete evacuation of the plant within 40 minutes. They also managed to locate and successfully rescue two workers trapped by the flames. Then they worked tirelessly for the next ten days putting the fires out.

How did it happen?

The cause of the disaster was traced to an incident two months earlier, when a crack was found in Reactor 5 at the plant. Workers fixed the problem by installing a bypass pipe, connecting Reactors 4 and 6. However, the new pipe was badly built and the fire on June 1 ruptured it, releasing about 40 tons of the chemical cyclohexane. This reacted with the air to form a highly flammable gas. After that, all it took was a spark to cause the largest peacetime explosion in British history.

The Nypro chemical plant after the explosion. By the time all the fires had finally been put out, 20,000 tons of flammable chemicals had been destroyed.

AT-A-GLANCE

Death toll: 28

Injured: 152, including 16 firefighters

Property damage: 90 percent of the plant destroyed; 100 homes in Flixborough badly damaged or destroyed

Seveso, Italy, 1976

It was Saturday morning at the chemical plant in Meda, northern Italy. In Building B they were producing a batch of the chemical dioxin. More heat was needed for the reaction, so they decided to use exhaust steam from an electricity turbine to help heat the reactor. As other parts of the plant began shutting down for the weekend, more exhaust steam was released, and the heat in the Building B reactor began to climb.

Toxic cloud

The rising heat went unnoticed by the few workers on duty. Just after midday, a valve broke. A cloud of chemicals, including the highly toxic dioxin, poured out of the building. The cloud rose high into the sky before being blown southeast toward the little town of Seveso.

BREAKING NEWS

July 20, 1976, Seveso …
Following an accident at a chemical plant in northern Italy earlier today, a cloud of toxic chemicals was released over the local area, causing alarm in the nearby town of Seveso. Some children have been treated for burnlike wounds. No statement has yet been made by ICMESA, the company responsible for the plant.

Children are treated in hospital following the leak from the chemical plant near Seveso. Many received skin lesions in the hours after the accident.

Food contamination

Within days of the accident, farm animals began dying. Thousands more were slaughtered to prevent them from entering the food chain. People living closest to the plant were evacuated, and everyone else was advised not to eat locally grown farm produce. In September, people in Seveso and other nearby towns began to suffer from a severe skin disorder called chloracne.

Italian Health Department officials inspect dead livestock on a farm near the chemical works. In the days following the accident, a total of 3,300 animals were found dead—mostly poultry and rabbits.

SEVEN YEARS ON

In 1983 five former employees of ICMESA, or its parent company Givaudan, were given prison sentences of up to five years for their part in the disaster.

Bhopal, India, 1984

It was 9 PM on Sunday December 2, 1984. At the Union Carbide pesticide factory in Bhopal, India, workers were cleaning the pipes above Tank 610. The tank contained a highly toxic chemical, methyl isocyanate (MIC), used for making insecticide. When mixed with water, it formed a deadly gas. But the workers knew the pipes were sealed. There was no chance of water getting into the tank...

Gas release

Sometime around 10 PM, a valve failed and water began leaking into Tank 610. The water reacted with the MIC to form a lethal gas. As the temperature and pressure inside the tank started to rise, workers were forced to release the gas to prevent the tank from exploding. At 12:40 AM on December 3, the gas burst out of the tank and began escaping from the plant.

Evacuation

The factory manager ordered the site to be evacuated. Workers, feeling the stinging vapors in their eyes, fled the plant. They headed north, as the breeze carried the gas cloud southward, toward the sleeping city of Bhopal.

SAVING LIVES

Even after the gas began to leak out, disaster wasn't inevitable. A filter system called a scrubber should have made the gas harmless. Secondly, a tower should have burned the gas as it escaped. Tragically, on that night, both of these emergency systems failed.

The ruins of the Union Carbide plant, photographed 25 years after the accident.

AT-A-GLANCE

Contents of Tank 610: 46 tons of MIC

Gas released: 20–40 tons

Temperature of tank at time of gas release: Approx 500°F (250°C)

Bhopal, India: Killer Cloud

The thick yellow gas was denser than air and rolled along the ground through the slums on the edge of the city. Many died as they slept. Others were awakened with severe burning in their eyes and throat. The air, survivors later claimed, smelled of hot chillies. Soon the streets were filled with hundreds of panic-stricken people, stumbling along blindly, desperate to escape the choking gas.

Night of tragedy

People had no idea where the gas was coming from. Thousands ran *toward* the factory and were quickly overcome by the fumes. One man's three-month-old son died in his arms as he ran. Another returned home to find his wife and children dead. The city's hospitals soon ran out of beds for the injured and dying.

EYEWITNESS

"The moment I took the rug from my face, my eyes started stinging and every breath was burning my insides."

Ramesh, a young boy living in Bhopal at the time of the disaster

Two people help a victim of the Bhopal chemical leak evacuate the disaster zone. Thousands were blinded or asphyxiated by the poisonous fumes.

Union Carbide

Around 3,800 died in the days following the Bhopal disaster, and up to 200,000 suffered injuries. Shock soon turned to anger when people discovered that Union Carbide, the company that owned the plant, had cut back on safety measures, repairs, and training. Five years passed before Union Carbide agreed to pay any compensation.

Local activists hold candles during a vigil on December 2, 2009, to mark the 25th anniversary of the gas disaster in Bhopal.

TWENTY-FIVE YEARS ON (AND COUNTING)

Since the Bhopal tragedy, around 20,000 people have died from injuries sustained that night. Many more struggle on with severe injuries to their skin and eyes. The factory, which closed in 1985, remained a contaminated site in 2010. Campaigners claim it is polluting local water sources and damaging the health of local people.

Schweizerhalle, Switzerland, 1986

In the early hours of November 1, 1986, people in Basel, Switzerland, were awoken by the sound of sirens. Looking southeast, they saw the night sky flickering red above the factories and warehouses of Schweizerhalle. The air was filled with the stench of rotten eggs and burning rubber. The local radio station warned residents to stay indoors.

Warehouse fire

No one ever discovered the cause of the fire that broke out at the warehouse at Schweizerhalle that night, but its effects would not be forgotten. The warehouse, which lay on the bank of the River Rhine, belonged to Sandoz chemical plant, and it contained pesticides, mercury, and many other agricultural chemicals. The fire took five hours to put out, and the firefighting water washed the chemicals straight into the Rhine.

Following the fire in Schweizerhalle, workers in protective suits start to clean up the burned-out Sandoz warehouse.

River runs red

Around 30 tons of pollutants entered the Rhine, turning the river red. Thousands of fish, eels, and water birds died in the days and weeks that followed. The chemicals flowed 540 miles (900 km) along the river, through six countries, and into the North Sea.

Dead fish are discovered in the Rhine following the chemical leak from the Sandoz warehouse. The river's eel population was almost completely wiped out.

SAVING THE ENVIRONMENT

The disaster prompted a clean-up campaign called the Rhine Action Program, which began in 1987. By 2000, it had achieved a 50-100 percent reduction in various pollutants. In 1997, salmon returned to the Rhine. By 2020, it is hoped that the river will be clean enough to swim in. Chemical factories by the river now have giant basins to trap water used to fight fires.

Toulouse, France, 2001

At 10.18 am on Friday 21 September 2001, the town of Toulouse was rocked by an enormous explosion. Two production halls at the AZF fertilizer factory lifted into the air and disintegrated in a ball of flame. All that remained of them was a crater 65 feet (20 m) deep and 650 feet (200 m) wide.

Shock waves

The shock waves from the explosion were so powerful they sent cars flying off the nearby highway and caused a local shopping center to collapse. Over a 3-mile (5-km) radius, windows were shattered, doors were ripped from hinges, and everything was showered with dust and rubble.

Two emergency workers walk through the skeletal remains of the AZF chemical factory following the devastating explosion and fire.

EYEWITNESS

"On the AZF site, there is only rubble. The factory buildings have been blown away. There's almost nothing left."

A witness to the explosion

Terrorism?

A cloud of dense orange gas, smelling of ammonia, drifted over Toulouse. The explosion caused panic on the streets. Coming so soon after the 9/11 attacks in the United States, many thought it was a terrorist attack. Schools, stores and offices near the factory were evacuated, and gas masks were issued in Toulouse. People were advised to stay inside and close their windows.

Human error

The explosion turned out to be an accident. Among the chemicals stored at the AZF plant was ammonium nitrate, which can explode when overheated. Investigations later revealed that another chemical was mistakenly placed in the same warehouse, and the reaction of the two chemicals caused sufficient heat to detonate the ammonium nitrate.

AT-A-GLANCE

Amount of ammonium nitrate stored at the plant: 330 tons

Death toll: 30, including a 15-year-old boy attending a local school

Seriously injured: 2,400

Light injuries: 8,000

A wounded woman wipes blood from her face near the site of the AZF plant. Many people—some several miles from the scene—were injured by flying glass splinters from the exploding factory.

Guangxi, China, 2008

Ma Dewen, chief of the Guangxi Zhuang firefighters squad, got the call just after 6 AM on August 25, 2008. A huge explosion had ripped through a chemical plant near the city of Yizhou. It sounded very bad. He immediately rushed to the scene to direct the rescue efforts. Twenty fire engines were dispatched, along with two bulldozers and nearly 1,000 firefighters.

Chain reaction

The firefighters arrived to find the entire factory ablaze. The plant produced highly explosive products such as acetylene and ethylene. The initial blast had started several other smaller explosions as tanks containing other flammable substances caught fire. Specialists in chemical safety treatment were hurriedly summoned to the site to remove flammable and toxic substances.

The chemical plant near Yizhou goes up with a bang. One local resident said the explosion felt like an earthquake.

EYEWITNESS

"With explosions continuing and a fire raging, it is quite treacherous for rescuers, since there are huge hidden dangers amid the blasts, along with leaks of toxic gases such as ammonia and formaldehyde."

Firefighter at the scene

The fight goes on

Despite these efforts, the explosions persisted until almost 1 PM. At its height, the fire covered an area of around 2.5 acres (1 ha). At around 5:20 PM, the five-story factory building collapsed. The blaze was finally extinguished that evening. Twenty people had died and around 60 were taken to hospital.

Gas danger

The explosion caused poisonous gases, such as ammonia and formaldehyde, to leak from the site, endangering neighboring communities. As a precaution, 11,500 local residents were evacuated from their homes. All had returned by the following afternoon.

A factory worker is rescued following the blast. Most of the injured suffered burns and fractures.

SAVING THE ENVIRONMENT

Following the explosion, engineers erected four dams to prevent pollutants from entering the local Longjiang River. Rescue workers successfully removed tanks containing 1,000 tons of alcohol, 2 tons of liquid ammonia, and 3 tons of liquid chlorine.

Learning the Lessons

Even when a chemical accident has been dealt with, the fires put out, and the local environment cleaned up, it's not the end of the story. Investigations continue, often long afterward, to discover exactly what happened and how to avoid similar disasters in the future.

The Seveso Directive

Many of the disasters described in this book led to safety improvements. For example, six years after the Seveso accident, the European Union adopted the so-called "Seveso Directive." This forced factories dealing with hazardous substances to introduce safety systems, emergency plans, and regular site inspections. This directive was strengthened and amended following the Bhopal and Schweizerhalle disasters.

Green chemistry

Today, many scientists are researching ways of producing the materials we need by using less dangerous substances. This field is known as green, or sustainable, chemistry. Green chemicals are designed to break down naturally after use, so they do not pollute the environment. They are also less flammable or likely to explode than many traditional chemicals.

The world as it is

For now, however, the chemical industry remains, by its nature, a risky business. Chemicals can be toxic and may react explosively. No matter how many safety rules are devised, human error and mechanical failure can never be entirely eliminated, and disasters will sometimes occur. That is why our emergency services must always remain on the alert, ready to act when the next chemical factory or warehouse goes up in flames.

A technician carries out an inspection at a chemical plant. Lessons from previous disasters have been applied and, today, most chemical plants are safer than in the past.

SAVING THE ENVIRONMENT

Today, chemical spills are cleaned up using a range of techniques:

• Small spills on land are cleaned up by digging up contaminated soil and moving it to a secure landfill site.

• Spills on water are cleaned up using floating booms and absorbent substances.

• New techniques include using bacteria or chemicals called oxidants to break down pollutants.

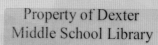

Glossary

absorbent Able to soak up liquid easily.

asphyxiated Deprived of air.

atom The basic unit of a chemical element.

consignment A batch of goods destined for delivery to someone.

contaminated Made impure by the addition of a poisonous or polluting substance.

convulsions Sudden, violent movements of the body.

electricity turbine A machine for producing electric power in which a wheel or rotor is made to revolve by a fast-moving flow of steam, gas, water, or some other fluid.

evacuation Removal of people from a place of danger to a safe location.

extinguish Cause a fire to go out.

fertilizer A chemical substance added to soil to increase its fertility.

flammable Easily set on fire.

insecticide A substance used for killing insects.

lesion A region in an organ or tissue that has suffered damage through injury or disease.

molecule A group of atoms bonded together. A molecule is the smallest unit of a chemical substance that can take part in a chemical reaction.

9/11 attacks An abbreviation for the terrorist attacks on the United States that took place on September 11, 2001.

pesticide A substance used for destroying insects or other organisms harmful to cultivated plants.

petrochemical plant A factory where substances are made by the refining and processing of petroleum or natural gas.

pollutant A substance that contaminates water, air, or land.

reaction (in chemistry) A process in which two or more chemical substances act on each other and are changed into different substances.

refinery An industrial establishment where a substance such as oil is refined (made pure).

reservoir An artificial lake.

respirator An apparatus worn over the mouth and nose to prevent the inhalation of poisonous substances.

rupture (of a pipe or tank) Cause to break or burst suddenly.

shock wave A sharp change of pressure in the air caused by an explosion.

synthetic Describing a substance that does not occur in nature, and has been made by synthesis (creating chemical compounds from simpler materials).

toxic Poisonous.

treacherous Hazardous due to hidden or unpredictable dangers.

Further Information

Books

American Disaster: Love Canal: Toxic Waste Tragedy by Victoria Sherrow (Enslow, 2001)

Disasters Up Close: Environmental Disasters by Michael Woods and Mary B. Woods (Lerner Publications, 2007)

Environmental Disasters: Bhopal: Chemical Plant Accident by Nicholas Bryan (World Almanac Library, 2003)

Rachel Carson: Fighting Pesticides and Other Chemical Pollutants by Patricia Lantier (Crabtree Publishing, 2009)

Toxic Waste: Chemical Spills in Our World by August Greeley (Houghton Mifflin Harcourt, 2002)

Web Sites

www.csb.gov

Web site of the US Chemical Safety Board.

www.dipity.com/timeline/Chemical-Plant-Explosions/list

A timeline of chemical plant explosions.

www.local1259iaff.org/disaster.html

An in-depth look at the Texas City disaster of 1947.

www.pollutionissues.com/Co-Ea/Disasters-Chemical-Accidents-and-Spills.html

An article describing the hazards of the chemical industry and how chemical accidents are dealt with.

timesofindia.indiatimes.com/india/Bhopal-Gas-Tragedy-Endless-nightmare/articleshow/5294330.cms

An article about the Bhopal disaster from *The Times of India*.

Index

Page numbers in **bold** refer to pictures.

acids 7
air pollution 6
ammonia 25, 26, 27
ammonium nitrate 8, 25
atoms 4, 30
AZF fertilizer factory 24, **24**

Bhopal, India 18–21, 28
BLEVEs 13

chemical factories 6, 7, 11, 14, 18, 22, 23, 24, 26, **26**, 27, **27**, 28
chemical industry 5, 28
chemical reactions **4**, 16, 25, 28
chemicals 4–5
chemical treatment plants 7
chemical waste **5, 10**
China 26–27
Chisso Corporation 10, 11
chloracne 17
compensation 11, 21
cyclohexane 15

deaths 6, 8, 9, 12, 14, 15, 20, 25, 27
dioxin 16

emergency procedures 6–7, 18, 28
environmental damage 6, 17, 23
European Union 5, 28
evacuation 6, 12, 13, 14, 17, 18, 25, 27, 30

explosions 6, 8, 9, 12, 13, 14, 15, 24, 25, 26, **26**, 27, 28

fertilizer 5, 8, 24, 30
Feyzin, France 12–13
fire department 6, 12, 14
firefighters 8, 12, 13, 14, 22, **22**, 26
fires **6**, 8, **8**, 9, 12, 14, **14**, 15, 22, 26, 27
flammable gases 8, 12, 15
flammable liquids 6, 26
Flixborough, UK 14–15
food contamination 17
formaldehyde 26, 27
France 12–13, 24–25

gas masks 25
Grandcamp 8, 9
green chemistry 28
Guangxi, China 26–27

High Flyer 9
Hungary 5

illness 6, 10
India 18–21
injuries 9, 12, 15, 16, **16**, 17, 20, 21, 22, 25, **25**, 27, **27**
Italy 16–17

Japan 10–11

liquid spills 5, 6

mercury 11, 22
methyl isocyanate (MIC) 18, 19
Minamata disease 11, **11**

Minamata, Japan 10–11
molecules 4, 30

Nypro chemical plant 14, **14**, 15, **15**

personal protective equipment 7, **7**
pesticides 5, 18, 22, 30
propane 12
property damage 8, 9, 14, 15

rescues 14
Rhine 22, 23, **23**
Rhine Action Program 23

safety measures 13, 21, 28
Sandoz chemical plant 22
Schweizerhalle, Switzerland 22–23, 28
Seveso Directive 28
Seveso, Italy 16–17, 28
site inspections 28, **29**
soil contamination 6, 29
storage tanks 5
Switzerland 22–23

Texas City 8–9
Toulouse, France 24–25
toxic chemicals 5, 7, **10**, 16, 18, 20, 22, 26, 27, 28

Union Carbide 21
Union Carbide factory 18, **19**
United Kingdom 14–15
United States 5, 8–9

warehouses 22, 25, 28
water pollution 6, 10, **10**, 21, 23, **23**, 27, 29